I0879246

NO GRAVE FOR THIS PLACE

No Grave for This Place

JUDY QUINN

TRANSLATED FROM THE FRENCH BY

Donald Winkler

Signal EDITIONS

THE POETRY IMPRINT AT VÉHICULE PRESS

Published with the generous assistance of The Canada Council for the Arts and the Canada Book Fund of the Department of Canadian Heritage, and the Société de développement des entreprises culturelles du Québec (SODEC).

SODEC Québec Canada

Canada Council for the Arts Conseil des arts du Canada

SIGNAL EDITIONS EDITOR: CARMINE STARNINO

Cover design: David Drummond
Photo of the author by Anna Quinn Nguyen
Set in Filosofia and Minion by Simon Garamond
Printed by Livres Rapido Books

Originally published as *Pas de tombeau pour les lieux*
© Éditions du Noroît, 2017

Dépôt légal, Library and Archives Canada and the Bibliothèque national du Québec, third trimester 2020.

LIBRARY AND ARCHIVES CANADA CATALOGUING IN PUBLICATION

Title: No grave for this place / Judy Quinn ;
translated from the French by Donald Winkler.
Other titles: Pas de tombeau pour les lieux. English
Names: Quinn, Judy, 1974- author. | Winkler, Donald, translator.
Description: Translation of: Pas de tombeau pour les lieux. | Poems.
Identifiers: Canadiana (print) 20200282832 | Canadiana (ebook)
20200282859 | ISBN 9781550655568
(softcover) | ISBN 9781550655605 (EPUB)
Classification: LCC PS8633.U57 P3713 2020 | DDC C841/.6—dc23

Published by Véhicule Press, Montréal, Québec, Canada
www.vehiculepress.com

Distributed in Canada by LitDistCo
www.litdistco.ca

Distributed in the U.S. by Independent Publishers Group
www.ipgbook.com

Printed in Canada on FSC certified paper.

CONTENTS

PROLOGUE

The moose at dawn crosses Highway 20 then
the strip of forest to the south that fronts the housing
complex and once on Alain-Grandbois Street
meanders between buildings his hooves
sinking into flower beds and rectangles
of freshly unrolled turf trashing
a swimming pool along the way from which he
extricates himself with difficulty three heads of family
are running behind him two of them with guns the school bus
stops on Lionel-Groulx five children climb on
the moose bleeding slips to its knees pulls itself up
the bus passes the three men
a girl sitting up front
starts singing *Three Little Kittens.*

There are days like that of utter dispossession
the carcasses drained
the hammering hushed
they take the child into their arms
each in turn with nothing said
she's not to look
little girl whatever you see
never forget
Auberivière
is shelterless.

One

Auberivière is a wide detour
there you learn to make cupcakes
to capsize toy boats
a security guard tells you a story
and the coming of a bird
raises high hopes
along with fear
will I be able to bear the journey
will something of me be left back there?

Auberivière commemorates Quebec's second
bishop whose life was cut short
by a fever contracted in the hold of a ship
two weeks of downfall on American soil
last hasty rites before dying
he would have said drink and eat
this is my body also go thou and multiply
which is what they did
and that's all they did
and that's it
for history.

On the way in you're strongly advised
to take an extra ticket
the magic might not operate right from the start
we weren't trying
to mimic others' insignificance
what you'll find here
is what's happening deep inside
the streets are landing strips
for planes that will never arrive.

Sani Mobile's chemical toilets
are on the corner going into the housing complex
their colours
correspond to multiple states of mind
but a mind state may not conform
to the colours of the toilets
by and large we prefer there to be no distinction
between surrounds and feelings
or between feelings
within a self or a group
the same night fractures but
different hands must carry out the mending.

It was before the streets had names of flowers
that on wedding invitations look so nice
the developer the city council the mayor
all supported the change
there'd be Tulips and Roses
and Lilies but not Carnations
though some people would still have to live
on Rina-Lasnier
like a tombstone that's done changing its name.[1]

[1]Rina Lasnier, *Mémoire sans jours.*

Along the streets the cedar hedges
are the woods' reprisal against what's human
the laboratory's window gives
onto darkness and tinder that burns
with misfortune's flame
but the tree's blind to the beauty
of a woman in a nightgown
breasts in ruin playing
in the ashes with a stick
the tree has its own take
on injustice and sacrifice.

The trees touch
respond to the movements of others
their most recent gestures imperceptible still
or indistinct
while it's the first stirrings
that define a tree's shape
so it is for the shadows
on the houses' north side
where children swing
going from dark to light
not grasping a single word
yet they're fearful
when their bodies swoop down.

There is nothing arbitrary
in the disposition of the white rocks
no one chose the colour
a girl wants something different on her head
clearly no one ever knew
how to dress her in proper clothes
might she then have had different thoughts
when the sky
darkened?

Among all the present tenses here
yours fronts the continuum
in a morning slow to recover
from a great debauch of nothingness
at the opposite end the dead descend
the steps of prefab houses
champagne flutes in their hands
trucks ply muddy worksites
it drizzles and it's cold
with so much horizon
in a single instant
she could in theory easily
raise her head.

In the evening she hears
an Asian volcano go dark
they've all forgotten her
in the past's décor
as in *The Twilight Zone*
except that heroes
wake
at forty past noon on the dot
in the future
no one here will ever recapture her.

What we call dead matter
is also capable
of representation according to Leibniz
who never visited however
626 Hector Fabre Street
to glue fake leaves
onto a plastic wreath
on a November night
the wreath
seems to be enjoying itself
but the house is sad
as are the lawn and the bicycle rack
and the young girl but she can do nothing about it
plastic wreaths are born every day
things don't ask for your opinion
nor that of other things.

She'd not yet opened her eyes
when Auberivière was already inside her
people and animals
are the utterances of things
a wreath could not be perturbed
like a dog thinking of the sun
threatening its little ones
there would be what's outside only
and this hole within oneself
the body would set the hole aflame
would clothe itself again for no reason
blessed be the day
that Auberivière hid itself away.

But the sky inside oneself
is no kin to the everyday
the cedar branches stir
on one side and the other
only those within
hoping to see where the gaze begins
never cease to grow
at the same time repelling the night
the night homing in on mortals
and making dogs howl.

You have to cross the housing complex
at least once
to get a sense of those circumspect rifts
as if there were space that could not be filled
or something were missing
that was there before
no one can explain
how this thing could have disappeared
or where it may have gone
we imagine red apples
falling then rotting
but things resist
becoming a void.

A race of dogs was invented there
one that doesn't yap or lick or drool
the new arrivals have neither fur nor tail
they devour you with their enormous eyes
while fires go cold
the little dog by the river
rolls in the stones
stops dead from time to time its muzzle dug in
the river with its backwash wants to lure the dog
wash it clean it of its musty smell
so will you proceed through many more mutations
before divining the wisdom they bestow.

Yes the void is not
at variance with matter
when with wet hair
her back flushed she chews
on her bathing suit's strap
with a weariness that's manifest
and frank
this is a face
at peace deep in the void
the precipitate of what
might have been.

Two

Once on a time crossing the park with its latrines
out of the woods a spring bored
a fault through the swamp
and when part of the fault filled in
the water sought another path
but like a bloody-minded goose
it now rams the earth
that nearer the houses
is not so forgiving.

Even fallen the trees keep growing
flattening pipes and poisoning the water
the children drink
the parents bring in specialists
the trenches fill with rainwater
that mirrors the dead trees
while the children fire up barbecues
as parents play in this forest
bury their faces
in a hole big as an ancient egg
flocks of crows overfly
Auberivière the fields then the highway
bringing sick animals home to us
the egg rolls in the trenches
a new dream is bruised every hour.

It's not a matter of seeing clear
to see is no bunker
nor is to hear and to smell
to smell and to hear might lead them astray
in the end they'll all be found.

But words do not match
what's happening
if you talk to people here
at all costs shun long explanations
that please no one when you get right down to it
it's not a religion they believe in
and if they do so it's involuntarily
just as they love
what's contrary to what they desire
in the end sorrow
is uncertainty
as for a potential complicity
between words and things
ideas and happenings
with a bit of good will
might mud set
more quickly?

Houses are an inadequate covering for the earth
cow bones are unearthed by children
every full moon a pack of cats
throws itself on the electric fences
surrounding our inner lives
and the animals howl for hours
hearts are too removed from the centre
it's always too cold or too hot
dogs it's clear have the wrong masters
whatever we make our own dispossesses us
the rain jells before our mouths
we are acting in farcical films.

How to be sure that the returning day
is really the day
the sky can't be changed like a dress
they ask the child
if the bird will suddenly stop flying
because it no longer believes in the sky
the child shows them how to slip between gravestones
but will not stoop to digging his own hole.

As for the rest tap a doll's arms
to find its vein
seek out the perfect network
the basements are full of old remotes
scraps of hosts and arms with sedating darts
the on and off switches no longer work
no one has yet touched
a stone's soul.

A hand slides the stone into a pocket
and takes pleasure in warming it
there is between hand and stone a fierce struggle
as between two starving men
a lamp speaks the language of lamps
why must we always
make our peace with stones
for a hundred grams of mouldy bread
and a fireplace
that spits day and night.

Armed drones overfly Auberivière
the soul is never wholly digested
Monday mornings beneath their patios
families suck on the crumbs of long gone revelries
what's left of the soul
is like a small hard orange
at the hub of a lonely arena.

Later there they are buck naked in a row
before a Sears cashier
not knowing what it's worth
to have lived for nothing
even with a dash of fury
and what it's worth having lost
and to be losing still.

On every side life
has turned insubstantial
threadbare
they have taken to their heels
electric wires dangle from the ceilings
in the streets a blood of steel
so much do they see through the scrim
of living that their footsteps
are cards
thrown down before sand
and the sand knows no end.

Auberivière has reached the maximum weight
the void might support
on its boundaries a landscape shrinks back
yet it would take up no space
no more than the vanished of whom we dream
and whose warmth we feel
when we press them close
but who are legion
blocking exits and entrances
such is their bodies' calling
this day will not dodge the eye.

Three

On the outskirts of Auberivière there is the mother
she repaints the asphalt and fixes her face
on her the rain doesn't dry
the child clings to her thighs
as to a dike
the streets are numbered 1 to 100
one must keep the ovens clean
tomorrow's not another day
so long as beauty makes for pain.

The Ultramar refinery casts a glow
as far as the riverbed
Auberivière is an eternal dawn
only wild animals confined
may reap profits from the moon
you rise at 2 a.m.
to the smell of leather
thoughts of revolution
and of matricide
to don reflective vests
as clouds like blotters
suck from the deeps
soured light.

Thursdays the classes in self-hypnosis
at the Galeries Chagnon they're playing *Love me Tender*
free samples of hand cream
with a purchase of fifty dollars' worth of brassieres
come with a fragrance of paradise lost
and there's no patent on this landscape
hands are so soft after
to think they've spent their lives
fondling the velvet of old car seats
at red lights.

The cars return ghosts to their bodies
a crumpled letter begins with these words
I waited for you but you didn't come
so I went in
and the cars roll over the letter
the sort of message you don't sign
don't know really where to set down
in front of the door or on the kitchen counter
with a glass of red wine
and its detectable lip prints
not present in police files.

What can you do
the noise knives make
never rouses the beast
as it will not awaken the tree
trapped in the wooden table
and fingers that crush
dry bread crumbs
feel like they're popping
street lights
down a road that never ends.

For ten years they've been gnawing away at the same
patio table without ever reaching the ground
the chairs don't go with the table
nor the mother with the daughter
once all was part and parcel
of a single solitude
it was a murky landscape
you couldn't tell people from fruits
the tables rotted like coffins
they suffered terribly as they ate.

Would like to merge with his house
so as to live in it
loves Chinese food
separated with three young
children
would have big windows
and a guest room
all digital communication
restricted
to two hundred and eighteen characters
in the main
out of concern for hygiene.

To grow up facing the broken branch
of an ornamental tree
does not confirm the existence
of that solitude the dream
too freely embraces
the mother weeps watching *Dynasty*
and the most intimate desires reside
in the peach walls
through the French window as it glides
the night slips in but the girl
does not despair and her mouth is closed.

To be and to think you are
don't mix
any more than look-alikes do
declares one of the ten best
books of self-improvement
whose author also produced
a naturalist saga
it's enough it's said
(but here the reading stops)
to drink three litres of water
a day and to make yourself
very fluid by focussing your attention
on your sphincters.

A sob resounds in the depths of laughter
sharing with grass
a very soft wind
but grass is still grass
and the wind drifts off
the grass-self genus
would like also to love.

Four

It's not that Auberivière had chosen him
to see it
he was Auberivière
that point
where two lines cross
that else
are like the deaths of bells
tolled by the wind
in a forsaken town.

For years the yards
were already filled with doors
moribund satellite dishes shovels
snapshots of married life
in Auberivière the stacked landscapes lose their leaves
it's dark under the sun
he'd only have to extend his arms
to unearth his own buried heart
clouds enfold
but do not conceal him.

It might have been worse
a man in and of himself
minus organs and skin
being denied a glass of water
as it's not like fire
to burn a tree halfway
the straw body awaits its hour.

Once upon a time the father found a blackbird
lifeless beside the road
this sight caused him no pity
or sadness
it just gave him pain
he was severed already
from luminous man.

At what phase of the amputation
do we find ourselves the father remembered
a house elsewhere that never existed
where he'd spent thirty years of his life
raised his children loved his wife
two or three streets from here
another man invented himself
went in to the office every morning
a Coors between his legs
suffering dug in its heels up ahead
where the signposts were red.

The house barely begun
but only in a certain sunset light
did it seem like a pile of rubble
in a compressed wood dumpster
the earth went rigid from cold
and as of then
a path never stopped shutting down
thrown back on its untamed state
no one passed along it ever
but in its footfall remembrances it lives on
like any road leading to ruin.

The jacket misplaced
the laughter the mindfulness
of his limits
what he lost made him
yet more himself
in the middle of his head
a birthmark
disclosed itself by dint
of polishing
he spoke
on bible paper
come down to them as dust.

The eyes work like a clock
over a calm smooth sea
it's Friday the thirteenth at one
the father does the breaststroke
behind the house
then shakes himself off in the sun
he loves bowling
long goodbyes on the porch
Pavarotti he says to the child
the world is flawed
we're not all in it
at the same time.

If the tree for example
could have two lives
a tree life and a bird life
a place where it goes in
and another where it comes out
but just one tree
filling all of space
there are places you never enter
but from which you emerge unclothed as if the tree
had lost
the bird it was to be.

In this dim cramped half-basement
where for the first time he made love
with that girl called Diane who
wanted no one to touch her face
and back farther in time and space
a little guy from Charlesbourg
son of an Irish mechanic sculptor in plasticine
to touching the thereafter when the cage
snaps shut, but this doesn't last
he feels a breath on his fevered chest
no matter if it comes
from before or after there is
an escape hatch in the wound.

A lake fumes in spring
the father carves a round in the ice
through which he draws his line
the leaves' hearts have ceased their beating
the beasts become
one great creature
the lake is deep
nothing narrows ever.

While the great black hole
gathers its lost child in
there is that other tiny hole
wherein
weakly
the body expends itself
eyes shine
like discontinued coin.

He would not have had to close his eyes
the eyes free themselves on their own
are divides for roofs uninhabitable
where chairs ricochet in shadow
shake your boots off on the rug
come in my love
it's late
the time to meet is already past
there is no grave for this place.

No one blows on the stars
but everyone here is oddly responsible
thanks to a broken thread
if only the star were free
it’s we who are adrift.

And the father's body remained impaled
soon only an image was left
decomposing on the stake
those witnesses' terrified faces
still within him
they had never before
been able to see themselves
(next to a silver watch).

Elsewhere people and things
but this is perhaps only a thought
labour differently from here
at disappearance
which is not always just the erasure of an image.

Five

How many such places exist
no end to the same first names
on the trees and the accident sites
with their distinctive scripts
relating particular fates
children flee
to the side of the highway
mirrored snares grab at their shoes
while they await their turn
to love and die.

The hunter shoots himself in the groin
a station a train to a distant town
opening drawers in a hotel
a salesman finds his own clothes
soiled in the usual places
at three o'clock the alarm
the taste of apples
a woman heaves herself down from bed
it's not a disaster
people can mimic the dead
and recite by heart
old answers
computing their score in their heads
the fissure is never
this side of the world
locks pop open
thanks to children's fingers
onto inner calcifications
at the very most we know these hallways
giving onto an end
where anaesthetizing rooms
leave us stranded.

Could the dream flush itself out
other than by talking to itself
through an intricate network of tumours
over steaming cauldrons
the vapour would be the same
the dream would go on growing
few objects fit the flat of the hand
this would not be one
but something like a glove
yet hold out your palm
the obverse of a dream
that has not yet spoken.

Sometimes they dream they are dreaming
then divorced from the first dream
they find themselves unmoored
and fall
it doesn't hurt
but they dread this drop
after all the times they've plunged
into a pile of autumn leaves
the tiny bits of skin they were
layer the furniture
their thoughts heavy with saliva
while they stare at you beseechingly
you of the first dream
who have broken so many bodies.

This routine of returning
to the bedside of the former patient
to seek the forest in the street
and the story of this wolf
each step taking it farther from his hand
in the end the gamekeepers killed it
and removed a bouquet of lilacs from its belly
to walk on two roads at once
the fire bites down from one end to the other
half way along the walk is suspended
from a blade of sky
that also burns at both ends
there is a mid-point
with no other extremity
than ashes
and all this holds firmly together
like a comet.

One carries a pail full of tadpoles
the other has lost the use of his spleen
the storm's back in the swamp
the tadpoles rot in the pail
there are houses so warm
that the heart bleeds
the brothers have the same face
like a party wall
except they're turned to the sky.

The wind rolls the children forward like foam
you can read all the earth's wounds in their faces
that's how Auberivière came to be
else what would the night rub up against
to feel its shape
before dying Auberivière is thought to have said
Lord deliver us from evil
one night a girl leaves her mother they bring her back
her throat cut to bathe in her blood.

A little drowned girl weeps over Auberivière's grave
in the parking lot between the school and the church
of the same name
because two deaths cancel each other out
children play dodge ball
their eyes blind to the grave
the losers line up against the wall
amnesic and aggrieved.

The children love and no longer know
how to come out from their scorched tents
without setting their future on fire
this girl will open the door to a boy
their organs will be made from soluble stuff
and here they do not dissolve.

EPILOGUE

On Hector-Fabre's asphalt the City
has writ Hector-Fabre large
so each will know for certain
that he is there where he is
after the street joined Kennedy Boulevard
foreign cars came
the other way on Nelligan-Émile, XF-Garneau
Grandbois-Alain just when the girl
had already put childhood behind her and people
in general no longer cared
what were the names of things as long
as they had gas for their cars.

Signal EDITIONS

Carmine Starnino, Editor
Michael Harris, Founding Editor

SELECTED POEMS David Solway
THE MULBERRY MEN David Solway
A SLOW LIGHT Ross Leckie
NIGHT LETTERS Bill Furey
COMPLICITY Susan Glickman
A NUN'S DIARY Ann Diamond
CAVALIER IN A ROUNDHEAD SCHOOL Errol MacDonald
VEILED COUNTRIES/LIVES Marie-Claire Blais (Translated by Michael Harris)
BLIND PAINTING Robert Melançon (Translated by Philip Stratford)
SMALL HORSES & INTIMATE BEASTS Michel Garneau
(Translated by Robert McGee)
IN TRANSIT Michael Harris
THE FABULOUS DISGUISE OF OURSELVES Jan Conn
ASHBOURN John Reibetanz
THE POWER TO MOVE Susan Glickman
MAGELLAN'S CLOUDS Robert Allen
MODERN MARRIAGE David Solway
K. IN LOVE Don Coles
THE INVISIBLE MOON Carla Hartsfield
ALONG THE ROAD FROM EDEN George Ellenbogen
DUNINO Stephen Scobie
KINETIC MUSTACHE Arthur Clark
RUE SAINTE FAMILLE Charlotte Hussey
HENRY MOORE'S SHEEP Susan Glickman
SOUTH OF THE TUDO BEM CAFÉ Jan Conn
THE INVENTION OF HONEY Ricardo Sternberg
EVENINGS AT LOOSE ENDS Gérald Godin (Translated by Judith Cowan)
THE PROVING GROUNDS Rhea Tregebov
LITTLE BIRD Don Coles
HOMETOWN Laura Lush
FORTRESS OF CHAIRS Elisabeth Harvor
NEW & SELECTED POEMS Michael Harris
BEDROCK David Solway
TERRORIST LETTERS Ann Diamond
THE SIGNAL ANTHOLOGY Edited by Michael Harris
MURMUR OF THE STARS: SELECTED SHORTER POEMS Peter Dale Scott
WHAT DANTE DID WITH LOSS Jan Conn
MORNING WATCH John Reibetanz
JOY IS NOT MY PROFESSION Muhammad al-Maghut
(Translated by John Asfour and Alison Burch)
WRESTLING WITH ANGELS: SELECTED POEMS Doug Beardsley
HIDE & SEEK Susan Glickman

MAPPING THE CHAOS Rhea Tregebov
FIRE NEVER SLEEPS Carla Hartsfield
THE RHINO GATE POEMS George Ellenbogen
SHADOW CABINET Richard Sanger
MAP OF DREAMS Ricardo Sternberg
THE NEW WORLD Carmine Starnino
THE LONG COLD GREEN EVENINGS OF SPRING Elisabeth Harvor
KEEP IT ALL Yves Boisvert (Translated by Judith Cowan)
THE GREEN ALEMBIC Louise Fabiani
THE ISLAND IN WINTER Terence Young
A TINKERS' PICNIC Peter Richardson
SARACEN ISLAND: THE POEMS OF ANDREAS KARAVIS David Solway
BEAUTIES ON MAD RIVER: SELECTED AND NEW POEMS Jan Conn
WIND AND ROOT Brent MacLaine
HISTORIES Andrew Steinmetz
ARABY Eric Ormsby
WORDS THAT WALK IN THE NIGHT Pierre Morency
(Translated by Lissa Cowan and René Brisebois)
A PICNIC ON ICE: SELECTED POEMS Matthew Sweeney
HELIX: NEW AND SELECTED POEMS John Steffler
HERESIES: THE COMPLETE POEMS OF ANNE WILKINSON, 1924-1961
Edited by Dean Irvine
CALLING HOME Richard Sanger
FIELDER'S CHOICE Elise Partridge
MERRYBEGOT Mary Dalton
MOUNTAIN TEA Peter Van Toorn
AN ABC OF BELLY WORK Peter Richardson
RUNNING IN PROSPECT CEMETERY Susan Glickman
MIRABEL Pierre Nepveu (Translated by Judith Cowan)
POSTSCRIPT Geoffrey Cook
STANDING WAVE Robert Allen
THERE, THERE Patrick Warner
HOW WE ALL SWIFTLY: THE FIRST SIX BOOKS Don Coles
THE NEW CANON: AN ANTHOLOGY OF CANADIAN POETRY
Edited by Carmine Starnino
OUT TO DRY IN CAPE BRETON Anita Lahey
RED LEDGER Mary Dalton
REACHING FOR CLEAR David Solway
OX Christopher Patton
THE MECHANICAL BIRD Asa Boxer
SYMPATHY FOR THE COURIERS Peter Richardson
MORNING GOTHIC: NEW AND SELECTED POEMS George Ellenbogen
36 CORNELIAN AVENUE Christopher Wiseman
THE EMPIRE'S MISSING LINKS Walid Bitar
PENNY DREADFUL Shannon Stewart
THE STREAM EXPOSED WITH ALL ITS STONES D.G. Jones
PURE PRODUCT Jason Guriel
ANIMALS OF MY OWN KIND Harry Thurston
BOXING THE COMPASS Richard Greene
CIRCUS Michael Harris

THE CROW'S VOW Susan Briscoe
WHERE WE MIGHT HAVE BEEN Don Coles
MERIDIAN LINE Paul Bélanger (Translated by Judith Cowan)
SKULLDUGGERY Asa Boxer
SPINNING SIDE KICK Anita Lahey
THE ID KID Linda Besner
GIFT HORSE Mark Callanan
SUMPTUARY LAWS Nyla Matuk
THE GOLDEN BOOK OF BOVINITIES Robert Moore
MAJOR VERBS Pierre Nepveu (Translated by Donald Winkler)
ALL SOULS' Rhea Tregebov
THE SMOOTH YARROW Susan Glickman
THE GREY TOTE Deena Kara Shaffer
HOOKING Mary Dalton
DANTE'S HOUSE Richard Greene
BIRDS FLOCK FISH SCHOOL Edward Carson
THE SCARBOROUGH Michael Lista
RADIO WEATHER Shoshanna Wingate
LAWS & LOCKS Chad Campbell
LEAVING THE ISLAND Talya Rubin
INSTALLATIONS David Solway
MOCKINGBIRD Derek Webster
LATE VICTORIANS Vincent Colistro
MODEL DISCIPLE Michael Prior
BASED ON ACTUAL EVENTS Robert Moore
STRANGER Nyla Matuk
SIREN Kateri Lanthier
TABLE MANNERS Catriona Wright
SIT HOW YOU WANT Robin Richardson
EAST AND WEST Laura Ritland
THE HARDNESS OF MATTER AND WATER Pierre Nepveu
(Translated by Donald Winkler)
AFTERWORDS Geoffrey Cook
THE SUICIDE'S SON James Arthur
WHAT WE CARRY Susan Glickman
ALL I HAVE LEARNED IS WHERE I HAVE BEEN Joe Fiorito
THE OUTER WARDS Sadiqa Meijer
NO GRAVE FOR THIS PLACE Judy Quinn (Translated by Donald Winkler)
LOST FAMILY: A MEMOIR John Barton

Véhicule Press